Introduction

Hello Ladies! If you are reading this then I am going to go out on a limb and assume that you are one of the millions of Americans who struggle to pay their bills each month. To put it frankly, you're broke! There's a lot of us broke girls out here so don't feel alone. I know it can be overwhelming at times living paycheck to paycheck. I know it can be upsetting when we cannot do the things that we would like to because we cannot afford them. I myself have cried myself to sleep at night because I didn't know how I would get gas in my car to get to work in the morning or what I would eat for lunch. It is not a good feeling and can sometimes be a never-ending cycle that just wont break.

Did you know that the average CEO-to worker ratio is 204/1? That means that the average CEO makes $204 for every $1 that their lowest level employee makes. Let's do some quick math shall we. Let's say you make $15 per hour and you work a 40-hour work week. Your paycheck will be approximately $600 at the end of the week (and of course that's before taxes come out). Now let's use the pay gap ratio to see how much the owner of the company made at the end of the same 40-hour work week. *Drumroll please:* $8,160. This pay gap is what keeps everyday workers in this cycle of poverty. Like seriously who came up with the idea that a $.50 raise every 6 months was enough. You'll be retired by the time you raise your salary enough for a vacation. (of course, I'm exaggerating but you get the picture) There are people who devote 20 years to a company and their pay still has not grown enough for them to improve their way of life. The worst part about these statistics is the fact that we ALL know the lower level employee works the hardest right? I mean how hard do you think the CEO works? The CEO is on the golf course while you're on your hands and knees scrubbing a toilet. And That Sucks....

So, if you are like me you've stayed up late and brainstormed a million ways to change your circumstances. The truth is that the only way to drastically change your circumstances is to drastically change your mindset. We must first recognize that we are working our fingers to the bone and the profit goes straight up to the top. Your salary is an expense for a business, so therefore you are a bill. I will use McDonalds as an example. The average McDonalds store makes $1808/day, which is $12,656/week. At the end of the week the bills must be paid, meaning the rent, water and gas and electric bill is paid, the food and other inventory is ordered, and the employees are paid. The amount that's left over after that store pays its expenses goes directly to the owner who has the power to determine if he/she will invest that money back into the business or pocket the money. I bet your wondering how a store can make $1808 per day and that stores full time employees wont even make that amount in one month. Somebody must tip the scale back in our favor, and that's where you come in.

The age of technology has shifted us into a new era, an era in which **anyone** can be a business owner. Social media and the internet have made it easier to get products and services directly to customers. 20 years ago, a business owner would need a storefront location or hundreds of thousands of dollars in startup costs to get a business off the ground. Today we can start a business and grow it from the ground up simply by advertising to our social media friends. We all have seen those "glow-up" stories of people that have changed their entire lives simply from social media. The possibilities are endless when it comes to what you can do to bring extra income into your household.

This book will be an interactive guide to helping you become your own boss. It does not matter the industry or the skills you may have, there is money out here for EVERYONE! It doesn't even matter how much money you have right now. (It wouldn't really be a book for broke girls if we were sitting on start up costs, right?) While this book will focus on helping you to choose and start one business idea I do not want you to limit yourself to one business. This could be the first stepping stone to you bringing in multiple streams of income. Once one business becomes profitable it is possible to use those profits to start another business. Once you have the basic knowledge needed you can take what you have learned and become a millionaire! This book was not written by someone at the top looking down but someone who has been exactly where you are.   I have gone through so many hurdles becoming a business owner I believe it is my duty to share what I have learned. If I could help one woman avoid going through half of what I've had to go through I believe this book will have been a success. So, grab a pen and let's take the first step to financial freedom together.

<u>Chapter 1: What Can You Do?</u>

I believe we were all born with our own special gifts, skills or talents. Those talents may be something you've known you could do from birth or it may be something you had no idea you could do. There are some people who have been singing or dancing their entire life. These people have discovered their talent at an early age. There are some of us who do not know exactly what our talents are and therefore we have tricked ourselves into thinking we were not blessed with our own talent. That is the biggest lie you can tell yourself.

I have always had a fascination with arts and crafts. I used to spend hours making scrap books, and I even taught myself how to knit one day just because I was bored. I cannot tell you how many times I have been in the craft aisle at Walmart buying something that I didn't need just so I could make something in my free time. I had no idea that decorating cakes would be in my future. One day I was going through a hard time, struggling to find out what my next steps would be after dropping out of nursing school. Right out of high school I picked an occupation that I believed would make an ok salary and I went off to college. I had no real passion for nursing even though I constantly told myself I wanted to be a nurse. 3 years after living in another state and going to nursing school, my family went through hard times financially and I had to move back home and get a job. It was while I was working this job that I stumbled into my gifts. I have always loved to cook, so one day a thought popped in my head that maybe I should go to culinary school. The next day I scheduled a tour of the local culinary school in my town. After the tour I had a strong urge to go after the baking and pastry arts program as opposed to the full culinary program. Now that I think back on that time I know that there was something calling me into my destiny. The first thing I noticed about the baking and pastry arts program was that at the end of the program the students got to make beautiful wedding cakes. I looked at some of the cakes that were made by past students and I was immediately blown away that something so beautiful could be made from cake. I went through my culinary school program learning how to bake bread and pies but secretly wishing that we could fast forward to the decorating term. It was just my luck that the term before I was supposed to start learning how to decorate, I learned that the school would be closing for good. I was devastated, and I felt like I had wasted my time. If this had not happened I would not have gone home one day determined to teach myself how to decorate cakes. I learned of my passion for decorating cakes simply by luck of my circumstances. This all happened only 4 short years ago. I can only imagine how far I would be had I taken the time to evaluate my skills and what I wanted to do with my life and I may have made my way to my calling sooner.

Like I said, I always knew that I loved to cook. I was the weird child who would sit for hours watching the food network channel instead of cartoons. I did not look at my cooking or my passion for arts and crafts as talent. When I made a few cakes for the first time and really started testing my skills I would look down at my hands amazed. I could not believe that I could look at a picture of a character and make that character out of fondant and sugar paste with virtually no training. I had no idea I could look at a cake and see exactly how it was made and recreate it. I spent years literally shocked when a cake I made came out looking great. I stumbled across my talents, but they were there all along I just didn't know how to find them. Sometimes life will throw you plenty of curve balls to get you to be on the right path. It wasn't until some years went by that I could truly see how everything had worked out to get me exactly where I needed to be. I was very upset with the direction my life had gone in and not being able to finish college with my peers. I now look at all these circumstances as hidden blessings. I cannot imagine how miserable I would be today as a nurse just going through the "motions" of a career I do not like. I want you to start thinking about some of the circumstances in your life. Does it seem like life is always pushing you away from something and towards something else? This may be where you are meant to be. I also want you to think about the things in your life that bring you the most joy. What do you go to when you're bored? What do you do to ease your mind when you're feeling anxious? I know someone who makes their own clothes on their free time for fun. If that is something you already do for fun that could be something you can turn into a business.

Use this space to write down 5 things that you feel you do well. It does not have to be something you are an expert at. (for example: I can bake, I can cook, I can draw, I can teach, I can sing, I can write)

1)

2)

3)

4)

5)

Use this space to write down 5 things that you find fun or interesting. These are the things that put a light in your eyes or make you happy but doesn't necessarily have to be a skill (for example: I love fashion, I love photography, I love making people laugh, I love cooking) *your interests and skills can be the same thing!*

1)

2)

3)

4)

5)

I want you to enjoy this easy part because it only gets harder from here. Remember I stated that there is money out here for everyone? Well, what if I told you that today you can make money doing absolutely ANYTHING! That means that your next business should be somewhere hiding in this list that you just made. The important part to remember is that the business does not have to be obvious but can be unconventional and completely out of the box. For example, if I love to cook I do not have to open a restaurant, I can also write a cookbook, start a meal prep business, become a private chef, or start teaching cooking classes. If I like to draw I don't have to limit myself to selling my drawings I can also start designing logos for businesses. It's time to be creative.

****Broke Girl Tip: YouTube pays! Any of your interests can translate to YouTube profit. If you chose cooking as an interest you should start a YouTube channel and record yourself cooking. If you like to sing you should be singing for your followers on YouTube. Not only does the platform pay real cash money but it brings the exposure and marketing needed to get a business off the ground. There is no downside to getting your gifts out the world!**

The main reason why I want you guys to choose your business idea from your skills or interests is because with the journey you are about to embark on it is very important that you love what you are doing. If love is too strong of a word you should at least *enjoy* doing it.   So many times, we pick our careers based on salary or convenience and then we stay in a job that makes us miserable. If you must drag yourself out of bed and force yourself to go to work, you know how hard it is giving your all to something that is not meaningful to you. When starting your secondary income think of your business as being an escape. When I first started my business, I was working as a baker at a grocery store. I went in every night and baked bread, muffins, rolls and donuts. I was not fulfilled but it was my fulltime job, so I had no choice but to drag myself in every night. One morning when I got off work I purchased a box of fondant and went home to attempt my very first decorated cake. That cake was terrible! But that cake made me realize I *loved* what I had just done. It turned into an obsession for me figuring out what I could make, getting better at leveling, learning how to stack multiple tiers, it was all so exciting for me that I knew I had found MY thing. I started selling cakes right away, which threw me into being a business owner before I even realized I was one. I made a lot of ugly cakes, but I was paid for every single one. The more customers I had, the better my cakes looked and the more I perfected my skills.

I would not recommend jumping out there the way I did because I did ZERO research and went a whole year before I realized I wasn't making any profit off my cakes. I have made countless mistakes on this journey to financial freedom, and I'm sure I will make so many more. I have experienced the pain of going into something and it completely failing. I have even gone through finding a business partner and having that partner steal all my money. (yes, we will get there) I've gone through all these mistakes in business, so I can attest firsthand to the difficulties that will arise on this journey. My job now is to ensure that other women are fully prepared and ready, so they will not make some of those mistakes. Of course, I'm sure you're going to make your own mistakes as well, but I can help to at least open your eyes so that you're cautious and aware of the potential mess ups ahead of time.

One of the biggest mistakes that some entrepreneurs make is thinking TOO big. I know what you're thinking don't look at me like that! I *want* you to think BIG, however you must also be realistic.   Your business goals should start small and gradually get bigger and bigger. This first step is only the beginning to how many businesses you can start and how much money you can make! If your passion is makeup and you can beat your own face like nobody's business, Hey Girl! Now, it may be your dream to have your own makeup line, however that should be put into a future goals' category. Producing your own product is going to cost THOUSANDS of dollars. We put that goal into the future category because we must start small to eventually be able to make that step. Money does not just fall from the sky. Your hard work on the small steps will determine if your future goals are even in reach for you. That is why you should start with being a freelance makeup artist. Use a small corner or a part of your home and start building clientele. The more your business grows the closer you will be to your goal! My future goal is to have a product or dessert mass produced in a grocery store. I know that right now that goal would be very hard for me to reach. So, I would like to run my bakery for some years first so that I can build up my experience, and my bank account to prepare myself for my bigger steps.

Starting small in a business gives you the opportunity to learn as much as you can about every aspect of your industry. You should look at this as your own personal college course. Being a business owner does not require a college degree, but it does require some background knowledge. Let's think back to the makeup artist example. If you are going to eventually be transitioning from a makeup artist to having your own makeup line, your years as a makeup artist are your college courses. That way when you go into a meeting to discuss producing your own makeup line you will know exactly what that would entail. If you go into the meeting without the knowledge or financials required to make that step you may lose credibility and look unprepared. Therefore, as you're working as a makeup artist you should be doing the proper research to learn as much as you possibly can about your industry.

Being a business owner also means you need to learn how to manage money, track and purchase inventory, budget properly, and keep your business afloat. These are skills learned over time running a business. Your larger steps will require you to understand every single aspect of a company. View every mistake as a lesson and use every day in business as a learning experience.

Use this space to write down your top three business ideas. The ideas will be directly correlated to your list of interest. For example, if one of your interests are writing, one of your business ideas could be writing your own book! (that one is mine so don't try to take it lol)

1)

2)

3)

       Once you have picked your top three business ideas it is time to do a little research. You will need to have at least a basic understanding of each of your three ideas before you proceed to the next step of picking your business. You will need to have an idea of what that business would need from you to get it off the ground. After you understand each business, you can determine if you have the time to devote to that business or if you even want to put in the amount of work required. You will need to understand how you will be getting your product or service to your customer from start to finish. If you are creating something and selling it, the questions you need to have answered are; how long does it take to make? How much will it cost me to make? How much would shipping cost if I need to ship? How much gas would it require if I am delivering everything myself? How am I going to gain clientele? You need to remember that in the beginning you will most likely be doing everything yourself. That means you need to determine if you have the time to devote to taking orders, taking calls, marketing and running social media ads on top of producing your product. Don't worry about the money or time that you have right now, in the next two chapters we will be focusing on the aspects of our lives that we will need to adjust to make this business happen. Work on researching all your ideas and really consider what *YOU* believe is the best decision for you and your life. The hard part is that I cannot pick your business for you. On the next page you will find an outline where you can jot down the most important details about each idea. The important questions you will need to answer are how much money this business will need in the beginning, and how much time a week will it require of me.

****Broke Girl Tip: Do all your research and prep work for your business WHILE you are saving! Do not wait until you have acquired your funding to start setting up your social media sites. You should have all your small steps accomplished while you are preparing to launch your business. There will be a checklist in this book to help you so don't worry I've got you covered.**

This is your brainstorming page. The internet has everything you will ever need to know about each of your business ideas. *Do Not* skip this step and pick the idea you like the most without doing research you will quickly regret not taking the time to research what you're getting into. Google each business idea to get an understanding of each.

Business Idea #1:

How much money will I need?

How much time will I have to devote per week?

Business idea #2:

How much money will I need?

How much time will I need to devote per week?

<u>**Business idea #3**</u>

How much money will I need?

How much time will I need to devote per week?

I am going to fill out one of these with a hypothetical business idea so that you guys will understand what you will be researching.

Business idea: opening an online boutique

How much money will I need: I want to start with 5 unique pieces of clothing that I know will sell quickly. Where will I get these clothes from? (aliexpress.com offers great deals on bulk clothing)

look up 5 hypothetical items you would like to sell in your boutique and write down how much they will cost. Figure out how many of each size item you will need to order to be able to fulfill orders without running out 1 item cost 6.99/unit I want 2 of each size to start (2 s 2 m 2l 2xl) that would be 8 items total which would come up to around $56. That means if you want to stock up on 5 items to start you would need roughly $280 for your inventory (assuming most of your items are the same price point) research how much it may cost to ship your items. Place a hypothetical price on your items to see how much profit you would be making from one item minus the products cost and how much it costs to ship. I would say you could get this business off the ground with as little as $500 this is with the bare minimum and does not include ordering business cards custom packaging and other add ons you might want to have that makes your business stand out.

How much time will I need to devote per week: Running your website, checking your emails, replying to customers, travelling to the post office, ordering inventory etc. how much time will it take you to complete this task each week. This business would most likely require about 10 hours of my time per week. Do in have an extra 10 hours a week to put into this business?

Every business will have a different answer for each question. A meal prep business may require more time from you because you must shop and cook for each of your customers. You may also need to cook food that isn't for a customer but shows what you offer. In the beginning you will need to show people what you can do which will require you to put money out to purchase food that you aren't selling. One decorated cake may take me up to 6 hours to complete. I cannot possibly make 10 cakes every weekend because I would not have the time. Keep in mind that each business is different and try to come up with a rough estimate for each of your business ideas.

Chapter 2: How much money do you have?

After you have brainstormed what each of your business ideas would require of you, you should be closer to picking exactly which business is the one for you. Now it is time to get into the deep dark secrets of your purse to determine how much money you are working with. If you're reading this book you most likely do not have money just sitting in your bank account just waiting to be spent. While there are always alternatives to get business funding or help with the financial aspect of your business, it is very important to understand your budget and make changes before embarking on a business venture. In this chapter you will be delving into your personal finances and budget and I will be using real life examples that I'm sure all of us can relate to.

First, we need to determine how much you make. If you have a full time or part time job it should be very easy to determine how much you make by looking at your pay stubs or deposit slips. Make sure that the amount you write down is the amount you bring home, after taxes and other fees are taken directly from your pay. We will be speaking in terms of monthly income because that is the easiest way to determine your income versus expenses. I want you to add all income including money that may be gifted to you, child support, or any other assistance as well. I want you to calculate exactly how much money you bring in each month and write it below.

My monthly income:

Next, we need to determine what you are spending your money on. We all have our fixed expenses that do not change such as rent mortgage utilities internet phone etc. fill in what you pay each month and add it up to get your total fixed expenses each month

Rent/ mortgage:

Utilities (gas, electric, water):

Phone:

Cable:

Car payment

Car insurance

Health insurance

Other:

____

Total fixed expenses:

The most dangerous expenses are those expenses that are not fixed. These are the things that we pay for each month that we do not usually calculate into our budget. We must put gas in our cars and buy groceries and toiletries each month, but we do not usually recognize how much we are paying for these things. In this category we are also going to add our luxuries. Luxuries are those things that we pay for because we may have a little extra money such as getting our nails done eating out or going out for drinks. When I first started my business, I was getting my nails and toes done consistently every 2-3 weeks. A gel fill-in is approximately $30, and a pedicure was $30 as well. At the end of the month I realized that I was spending $120 per month on just my nails. I was also going to the salon to get my hair washed and blown out every 3 weeks which was $75. I could not believe that I was spending almost $200 a month on just my hair and nails. I want you to try to determine what you've been spending your money on. It may help you to look at your actual bank statement because it lists exactly what you have swiped your card for. This calculation does not have to be exact, but I want you to try to get an approximate amount of money you spend on each item per month.

Gas/Commute:

Groceries:

Fast food:

Drugs/alcohol/cigarettes:

Grooming:

Shopping:

Eating out:

____

——

Total sliding expenses:

If you're like me, you were most likely shocked by the last list you made. When I first realized how much I was spending on gas each week I was speechless. The reason gas is not a fixed income is because we never really know how gas prices are going to change. One week you may spend $40 on gas and the next week you may spend $60. Even at $40 per week you would be spending $180 per month on gas alone. I can easily spend $250 at the grocery store and I'm only feeding a family of three. Those groceries may last my family 3-4 weeks. I also know that I'm going to stop at burger king and taco bell when I don't feel like cooking or treating us to a pizza night when we want a special treat. Pizza night alone can come up to $25. I also would like to enjoy a nice bottle of wine or something stronger once and a while, which can add up faster than we can finish the bottle. The next equation will help you determine how much money you have at the end of the month to save for your business. If your number comes out to be zero or in the negative do not panic, this just means we have a few changes to make and you will be saving $100 a week in no time. Complete this equation to determine how much money you have available to save each month.

Total monthly income - Total fixed and sliding expenses = Amount you can save

Amount you can save:

The word of the day is SACRIFICE! Say it with me, *SACRIFICE!* That's right, if you're going to start on this journey I told you we would be drastically changing the way you think. When I realized I was spending almost $200 a month on my hair and nails, I had a decision to make. Were my nails being done worth all that money? I had to figure out if there was a way that I could reduce this expense so that I could save the extra money each month. My nails expense was the very first thing I cut completely. It was not that hard for me because I bake for a living, so I originally cut my nails and stuck with my pedicure. Eventually I started buying nail polish from Walmart for $3 and painting my toes when I needed them done. That small sacrifice saves me $200 a month. I decided that the hair salon had to be cut as well. For some of us the hair salon is a necessity (you know who you are) but luckily, I have always been good at doing my own hair or getting my sister to do my hair for free. I did have to spend money on my own shampoo and conditioner and styling products but that one purchase eventually saved me another $75 a month.

It is very important to separate the money you are saving every month so that you will not spend it. There are a ton of different ways to do this, so you can find the way that works best for you. What worked for me was utilizing my savings account. I learned early on that most bank accounts have a limit of how many times a year you can transfer money from your savings account to your checking account. I used this feature to my advantage by transferring the money into my savings account and knowing that I would not be able to touch it. There were those times when I didn't have any money and quickly transferred $20 over, but I tried to limit transfers to emergencies and if I absolutely had to transfer money I only transferred a small amount. The other way to save is to get some type of jar or piggy bank. Write the word

GOALS on a jar and start putting your extra money into the jar that you know you will not touch it. This process will take determination on your part because its very easy to go into your savings so much you look up and haven't saved anything. You must remain focused on your goal!

We all have different things we are willing to sacrifice. Can you commute to work to save on gas? Can you sacrifice going out for drinks or eating out for 6 months to reach your goal? You must determine what you are willing to give up changing your circumstances. There can be no progress without some type of change happening. I know a lot of the time our luxuries are the only things we have to look forward to out of our paycheck. I know it gets lonely staying in and watching everyone else go out and enjoy life. I have felt this way for many years, so I am here to tell you that feeling will not go away. There will be days where you simply cannot take the "sacrifice" any more. You're going to look at your friends and think "why can't I go on vacation". You must be mentally prepared for your friends to try to force you to come out. You must mentally be prepared for the days that you think "I've saved enough I'm going to treat myself". And do not get me wrong you CAN treat yourself but try to keep the spending to a minimum, so you do not disrupt your savings.

If you are able to remain consistent you can put this process into action for as little as six months. After six months you should be able to count your money and evaluate how far you need to go. If you were able to save at least $200 per month you should have $1200 that you are ready to devote directly to your business. Later we will talk about bridging the funding gap through credit, crowdfunding etc., but first, we have another aspect of our life we must adjust before we are ready to start our business.

Chapter 3: How much time do you have?

Time is not our friend. There are only 24 hours in one day. That means that if you want to start a business you have to be prepared for the amount of time you will need to put into your business. In this chapter we will be looking at your time as if it is money. After all, the more time you can dedicate to your business the more money you will bring into your business. Also, your time is not free! Your time is valuable and should be worth something. As I said before it can take me up to five hours to complete one decorated cake, and that's not including the time it took taking the order, shopping for the order and baking the cakes. Now I could price my cakes based on how much I need to spend to make the cake, but that would not be an accurate depiction of what I deserve. I deserve to be paid for the five hours of my life that I devoted to that cake. You should already be thinking about what you think your time is worth. Of course, you will not be making your "worth" right away and that's why the beginning of this process is comprised of a lot of working for free. However, it will pay off, I promise.

Since we are looking at your time as being equivalent to money we will need to calculate what you are doing with your time. We will keep the time frame small and come up with an estimate of what we do with our time each day. I want you to start thinking about what you do with your 24 hours. If you work full time, 8 or more hours of your day is devoted to your full-time job. If it takes you 30 minutes to get to work and back home, you should add another hour. It takes you approximately 1 hour to wake up, shower and get ready for work so you have already gone through 10 hours of our day. The average person should get between 6 and 8 hours of sleep per night so lets just go ahead and take that number up to

18. That leaves us with 5 free hours every day. Of course, there are some of us who work 12 hours per day or work 2 jobs. Use the next section to try to calculate exactly how you spend your 24 hours.

<u>Time spent</u>;

Working:

Sleeping:

Commuting:

Grooming:

Social media:

Television or internet:

Naps or lounge time:

____

Total:

24-Total=

How many hours per day do you have to devote to your business. If the answer is 4-5 then you are on the right track and should have enough time each day to sit at home and work on *something* related to your business. If you have less than 3 hours a day to give to your business, you should be thinking about making a few changes to ensure that you are not about to lead a zombie like existence with absolutely no sleep. Most of us are always on social media and if were being honest with our selves we have watched 2 hours go by as we lay in bed watching cat videos or on the shade room. We have all been there. The trick to taking control of your time is to make the smallest of changes first. For example, if you're like me you love reality tv. While the real housewives of Atlanta are on I am always tuned in. There are at least 15 minutes of commercials for every 1-hour show. Make the conscious decision to pull out your laptop, notebook, or phone whenever a commercial comes on and try to get one thing accomplished. After 2 hours you have taken 30 minutes of your free time to be a business owner! With such a small change in your routine you have put 2 and a half hours of work that week into your goals.

The same can be said with social media. We haven't gotten into creating social media accounts yet however when you do have your pages set up you should be browsing liking and posting from your business pages. It is important that the followers and friends you already have are in the loop with what you are trying to do because these people will be your first customers. If you have been practicing your craft, you need to start posting photos of your work before your business launches. This technique will peak your followers' interests. If someone sees that you made something beautiful and compliments you on it, they will most likely be willing to buy it from you when the time comes. You can also build up the anticipation by giving your followers something t look forward to. "Business launching soon" posts also get your followers excited or at least intrigued that you will be launching a business regardless of what the business is. You must also make your page public NOT PRIVATE and follow people that are not in your immediate circle. When I first created my business page I followed every single person I saw. Instagram eventually would stop me from following any more people and I needed to wait until the next day. If you want money you will not be afraid to get yourself out there in any way.

Since you agreed to *sacrifice* going out at night to save money, it's a bonus that you are saving your time as well. Every time you lay around doing nothing or go out socializing you should check yourself. The first thing that I do is think about what I could have done in that amount of time. I was at happy hour for 3 hours I could have been replying to all my emails. I took a 4-hour nap today, but I could have gotten another chapter of my book done. (don't say one word!) The one thing you must start doing is holding yourself accountable. Recognize when you're being lazy or when you're procrastinating. I know its hard for us to hold a mirror to our own lives but we can often be our own worst enemy. That's why you should be the first person to call yourself out when you aren't as disciplined as you should be. That does not mean that your business will not be successful, but I can guarantee you will learn that lesson whether you check yourself or someone else checks you. You will become overwhelmed when your tasks pile up on you, so its better to try to get things done when you have time. If for nothing else other than save you the headache and chaos that will ensue.

I remember when I decided to sacrifice eating out it was a horrible experience. I am the type of girl that loves fast food. When I was pregnant I would literally eat one item from every fast food chain I could think of. Anyway, there was a time when I was trying to open my store and did not have enough money. My sweetheart of a boyfriend watched me cry my eyes out one day and then said, "well didn't you just spend $20 at chipotle today"? needless to say I was *pissed.* Like how dare he call me out for spending money every single day on food and then crying about not having any money. I knew he was right, but the blow to my pride and ego of having someone from the outside looking in notice that I wasn't willing to sacrifice anything for what I wanted was eye-opening. After that I apologized of course for the temper tantrum I threw, but I also vowed to myself that I would make better decisions. I am not perfect and when I am in a rush I STILL roll on through that drive-thru, but I make one decision every day that will make a big difference in the long run. If I'm on my way to work ill grab some breakfast from the fridge instead of stopping for breakfast. I started making my coffee at home to stop the temptation of ordering breakfast with my morning coffee. I started packing lunch or cooking enough dinner to have leftovers. Now I have enough self-awareness to recognize when I'm doing something that is not beneficial to me or my business and I make the necessary corrections. A sign of maturity is recognizing flaws and changing bad behaviors. This is not an overnight process but being a business owner requires you to…. grow up.

Use this space to write down some of the things you think you could change about either your money or your time. Brainstorm the things you think you can get done if you implement these changes. I also want you to reflect on some of the negative traits you may have that you need to change as well. Short tempered, lazy, prideful, greedy, irresponsible? Be honest with yourself! Write the words and then draw a line through each one! Those traits MUST go.

<u>**Chapter 4: Picking Your Business!**</u>

Now that you have made the appropriate changes to your life it is time for you to pick exactly which business you will be embarking on. Some of you have had your idea already picked after the first brainstorming phase. If you have already picked which business, you would like to start then I am going to let you know what research you should be doing to get a better understanding of that business. If you have not picked your business yet, each of these steps will bring you closer to making your final decision. You should have a broad understanding of how much time and money each business will require you to devote to it. You can decide this by thinking about your work week as it relates to your business. If you work fulltime on weekends but you need to ship orders you may not have the time to make it to the post office. If you would like to be an event planner, you must understand that most parties are on weekends. If your job does not give you weekends off it would be very hard for you to devote your time to your event planning business. You may also find that you can make minor adjustments to your schedule to factor in your favorite business idea if it is still the most appealing for you. If your business will require you to answer calls from customers but you cannot take your phone into work with you for 8 hours you might want to consider a business in which daily customer contact is not necessary. Again, I can not make these choices for you, however I want you to be fully prepared to take on this new venture.

If you are already narrowing down your search then you may already be planning out what a typical week for you would look like with this extra load, and that is smart. After all we are sacrificing time and money, but we do not want to sacrifice sleep or sanity. A burnt-out business owner is not beneficial to anyone. Do not let this journey cause you to alter your life in a way that is not healthy for you! I cannot stress this point enough. When I was working overnights I also had a 2-year-old son. I would work from 11pm to 8am on a Friday night and have 3 cake orders waiting for me to complete when I got home. Safe to say I was utterly exhausted. I started getting headaches and feeling very overwhelmed. This caused me to be so mentally drained I considered giving up on my business multiple times. You must protect your peach of mind, it is the only way you will stay motivated. When picking your business do not bite off more than you can chew. Pick the business that will merge into your lifestyle and allow you to still rest and spend time with your loved ones.

The next step is to research your favorite business idea thoroughly! That means its time to be a little creep. As I told you before the internet has so many answers at our fingertips we just need to know where to find those answers. At this step we will be researching our competition. You should do a search for multiple businesses like the one you would like to open. Find their social media pages and look at how they are getting their product out to their customer. Notice how they are marketing and if you personally feel like that marketing is effective. For example, if you are starting a meal prep business you should see who else is offering meal prep services in your area. View their page to see if you can find out their prices. It is normal to seek out the prices of your competition to see where you will fall in price range.

You do not have to line your prices up with your competition, however customers do compare prices when deciding which business to support. If another meal prep business offers one week of meals for $59, it may be beneficial for you to keep your prices in that price range. However, if you feel you will be offering a better-quality product, larger portions, or an overall easier experience for your customer you may be able to price your services higher than your competition. They key here is to know that if your prices are higher than your competition your marketing needs to be tailored to explaining to your customer why they are paying a higher price.

When I first started, my prices were significantly lower than my competition. At the time I was not very confident in the quality of my cakes. I had a bad habit of doubting myself even when some of my work looked the same if not better than my competition. I would have customer tell me that a bakery wanted to charge them $900 for a cake I was charging $300 for. In the beginning this was beneficial for me building my clientele. Eventually I started to have more confidence in my work and I needed my prices to reflect that. I was effectively cheating myself out of more profit. I had to build my confidence to know that my work will be amazing, and I should be paid accordingly. Now my prices are still slightly lower than my competition, but I believe this keeps more clientele coming through the door. By looking at your competitor you can learn what you admire, what you do not agree with or what you feel you will do differently in your business.

It is important to remember that ethically you should never outright steal anyone's marketing strategies or ideas. Big corporations practice dirty marketing all the time. I know you have seen a commercial when burger king is blatantly coming for McDonalds. Recently Wendy's has started criticizing McDonalds for their frozen patties being used in their stores. It may seem funny to see two franchising battle for customers but in small business this could hurt your business. You should remember that you are just starting out and you want to establish yourself, you do not want to be a copy of another business. Now the exception to this rule is distance. If there is a business in California that you admire, and you are in New York it may be ok to take a few tips from that business that you love because if it is effective for them it will be effective for you as well. Be careful with getting on the bad side of local competition. You do not know how far any business owners reach is in your city. Especially businesses who have been open 20 years or more, they may know congressman, health inspectors, or future customers in general on a personal basis. Negative word of mouth can kill a business before it gets off the ground. Especially in this age when social media can make anything go viral and reach thousands of people. Imagine stealing someone's idea and they make a post calling you out and now you're the laughing stock of the internet. That would be a disaster.

During this research phase you are learning how you want to run your business from start to finish. This means if you are a hair stylist, you may see that some other stylists require their appointments to be booked through a site with a $50 deposit. You might think that booking through a site would deter potential customers because some people would like a more personal experience. This is where you are deciding what will work best your YOU. You may also notice that certain stylists have a ton of rules for their customers. As a consumer you may be turned off by the idea of someone laying out ridiculous rules for their customers. You then can decide that you don't want to be that type of owner. It is important to think like a consumer in this process. What stops you from supporting someone? How do you like to be treated when placing an order? If you require a business to ship your items in 3-5 business days, you know how important it is for you to incorporate fast shipping into your business model. If you think it is unprofessional for a business to not reply to your message in the first 24 hours, then you should make a rule that you will reply to your customers promptly.

This process should not stop either. You should start following other businesses in your field in other states. Start noticing what other people in your industry are doing right or wrong. You should also visit different sites where people in your industry are communicating or sharing notes. I have googled a question such as "how do you get your cakes level?" and found sites where other bakers are sharing their tips and tricks. It is cool to see a community of people who are going through the same things as you. I know there are certain cake decorators that I love to follow on Instagram. When there are funny memes that only us bakers will relate to someone will post it and we all share a laugh. We compare tips and complement each other's work. These bakers also keep me on top of my game. When I see how beautiful their work is it makes me want to work harder and get better. On the other hand, I do follow other bakers that teach me what *not* to do. I have seen other decorators go viral arguing with their customers or being completely unprofessional. I decided early on that customer service was one of the most important aspects of my business. I always try to remedy bad experiences whether they are my fault or not. I give away free products or give refunds before I allow a customer to leave my shop disappointed. The same way a business owner can bash you online a disgruntled customer can do the same thing.

A lot of people believe the customer is always right but sometimes customers are wrong. It is your responsibility as a business owner to remain professional and non-confrontational and fix problems before you lose customers. if you do not have great people skills it may be beneficial for you to pick a business in which you do not have to have direct contact with customers daily. Only you will know your flaws and you should identify those flaws and honestly determine how those flaws might arise while operating your business. I am very antisocial and usually do not like being bothered by people constantly. Those flaws go completely against what I need to do for my business. The way I have learned to cope with this is to let my customers know that all messages will be responded to within 24 hours. I have gotten texts for cake orders at 1 o clock in the morning, seriously. I am not rude, but I simply will not reply until the next day when I feel like replying. If I reply within 24 hours I have fulfilled what I promised to my customer. I know that there are some of us who would have sent a text back stating "my business hours are from 8-6 please do not message me this late again". I personally would not shop with someone who sends me that message. I think it is better to avoid confrontation and if I do miss a message or are late replying I immediately apologize regardless of how rude the customer has been. Sometimes you must humble your attitude to make money. Do not let your bad attitude chase your customers away. This business model has paid off for me because 85% of my customers are returning customers. I have clients who come to me around birthdays every single year. If your customers do not return they did not have a good experience.

If you have examined all the aspects of what your business will entail it is time for you to pick. Think long and hard about which business you can turn into a success. Be realistic and aware of the amount of work you are about to need to put into this business. Do not pick a business that you know for sure you will not be putting you all into. Starting something that you will give up on halfway through is unacceptable. Each business you start you should be ready to give your all to it. I believe it is not official until it is in black and white so next we are going to write down our final business idea that we will be launching soon. If you're indecisive write it in pencil and go through this research phase for all your ideas to narrow down again which one is a better fit for you.

My final business idea:

<u>**Chapter 5: The First Steps**</u>

Before your business will be ready to launch there are some basic background steps that you will need to set up. You must register your trade name and obtain all business licenses needed for your specific industry. These steps are essential to your business running professionally and smoothly when you do launch. When your business takes off you want to already have your website set up, emails set up, and a business bank account. It is important to separate your business funds and personal fund immediately. Imagine the panic you would have if someone paid you for an order and it goes into your personal account and then your phone bill comes out of your account that night. Yes, I have been that girl holding up the checkout line because my card was declined. I have also had to borrow money just to complete someone's order because the money had already gone to something I needed to pay. Hopefully, you will learn from my mistakes and follow these directions to avoid potentially damaging your business. Customers also like to feel secure about what they're spending their money on. If you sell something online especially, customers will always click your website first. If they go to your page and you do not have a website, do not have an email for contact or a phone number, you have lost a potential customer. This chapter will focus on each step you need to take to lay the building blocks of your business.

What is your business name? The name of the business is one of the most important first steps. This will require some research on your part because you will want to be original. Each state has a website that will list all the registered business names in your state. You should go to this site to confirm if the names you are thinking of are already being used by someone else. While this website is helpful you should not stop there. There may be another business in another state with the same exact name.

While it is not illegal for two businesses to have the same name, it can be confusing for the consumer. You also must remember that you will be creating and purchasing a website domain name. If another business already has your name their website might come up first in internet searches. You should search the name that you are looking for on Instagram, Facebook, twitter and website to make sure no one is running a site with the same name. Once you are sure you have an original name for your business you must act fast. I know the odds of someone snatching your name up as soon as you think of it is not very likely, but it does happen. The last thing you want to do is register your trade name and then realize there is someone running an Instagram account with your business name. You should first register your trade name with your state. My city has a business portal that literally lets you go through every step that I am laying out in this chapter. I am sure other states have websites where you can register your business as well. Make sure you have researched your states requirements regarding opening the business you are embarking on because some of those steps may be specific to your industry. There is going to be a cost for almost every item in this chapter, but the costs are small and can be handled one at a time.

After you have registered your business name you must go to the IRS website and create an EIN number otherwise known as a tax ID number. This number is considered a social security number for your business. Did you know you can build business credit? This number will be asked of you when applying for anything, or when opening an account at a bank. There is no cost for creating a business EIN and it does not take long for you to fill out the form and receive your number. An important tip is to invest in a printer and purchase a folder. You will want to print out your registered trade name as well as your tax id number for your records.

The next step is for you to decide how you want to legally organize your business. A sole proprietorship is a business model in which you are the sole owner of the business and will be filing the business on your personal tax return. If your business is a sole proprietorship you will always need your registered trade name as a form of verification especially at the bank. An LLC is a limited liability corporation. While filing your business as an LLC is not required, I have always been taught that it is the smartest way to set up your business. If you own a sole proprietorship business and someone decides to sue your business, they are suing YOU! There would be no way for you to separate your personal finances from your business finances and that person could come after taking your personal assets like your home. An LLC separates your business from your personal finances. If someone was to sue your business the worst that could happen is your business closes. You would be able to dissolve that business and move forward to start another without affecting your own life in the process. Filing your business as an LLC usually costs around $100 depending on how soon you would like to receive your articles of organization. There is also an annual fee that must be paid to keep your business in "good standing" in your state. In Maryland this fee is $300/year to keep your LLC registered with your state. If you would like to open a business bank account, you will need this paperwork with you, so you may need to pay more to have your paper expedited. Yes, I sat in the bank for 2 hours only to realize I had filed for my LLC but had to wait 2 weeks to receive the paper in the mail. Your city or state should have an office that you can go to and physically organize your business, or you should be able to do so online as well.

After you have filed these papers you are ready to open a business bank account. There will be no better feeling than leaving the bank for the first time after opening that account. It will feel even better if you have saved a large amount of money and you take that to the bank with you to make your first deposit. *Woooooooooooo* you will be smiling from ear to ear. I want you to enjoy these little accomplishments. Even with just these few steps completed you are a business owner! Celebrate your milestones whether they're big or small. This will keep you motivated and remind you of how far you have come. 5 years later you will remember opening your account, I promise.

The next steps are simple but time consuming. You will need to first create a business email address. The email address should be simple and professional. Anything other than yourbusinessname@gmail.com could be confusing for your customers. Take this time to create every social media site you can think of as well. This could be time consuming so grab a glass of wine and fill out those forms girl you can do it! Do not worry about decorating or pictures or logos or anything yet because it will take time for you to come up with consistent branding across all platforms. Set up your pages and go back as you get time to design them to look exactly how you want them to. I would recommend designing your website and logo first before designing your social sites. If your business will not have its own physical address, you can purchase a p.o. box so that all mail or correspondence for your business is going to the post office and not to your personal home. Purchasing a P.O. box will cost you around $25 so be prepared to pay this fee when you go to the post office.

Now it is time to purchase your business domain name and create your website. certain websites like GoDaddy.com will allow you to design your webpage and purchase your domain name at the same time. Wix.com is another easy website designing service, and this is the website I currently use. I designed my webpage in one day by myself after finding out how much other people were charging to design a site for you. My domain name cost me $11 for one year and my website costs me roughly $22 a month. Make sure you always keep your website up, if your bill is due it should be the first thing to be paid because a down website is not a good look for your business. Keep in mind that you do not have to launch your website at this stage, you can pick a date and do a "grand opening" to launch your site. It's your business and at this stage you can do with it what you want.

Broke Girl Tip: DO NOT pay anyone to do something that you can do yourself! When I opened my store, I turned into a painter contractor and a plumber. It

took me 2 weeks to paint my entire store myself. I purchased the paint at Walmart and brushes and went in everyday to paint. I would have paid someone almost $1000 to paint my store for me and I did it myself for free. This is called "sweat equity" meaning you are putting your actual sweat into the business and not just money. If you are good at computers and used to design your old myspace page there is no reason you cannot design your own website in one day! Keep your money and spend your time. It will pay off in the long run.

This would be a good time to pick the actual look of your business as well. That means that you should be picking colors and fonts and start designing a logo. There are websites like Vistaprint.com or logomaker.com that will allow you to create a logo on their site and you pay to download the image and keep the digital logo. You can put that logo on anything. These websites will have pre-designed templates that you can edit to create a personalized logo on your own for as little as $10. If you have extra money in your budget, you can look for a graphic designer who can design a unique logo for you as well. This is where you can be creative and make your brand reflect your personality and vision. Your logo and colors can then be inputted to every single one of your social sites as your main profile photo. This will create a consistent look and will be the start of your brand. You can always rebrand yourself as often as you'd like but try to keep your social sites consistent. You can also input all the other information that you now have such as your email address, and website into the bio of your pages so that people will know how to easily contact you.

After you have set up all these things your business if officially created! You are technically ready to get your business of the ground, but the last chapter probably hurt your pockets, right? The next chapter we will be talking about bridging the funding gap so that you will have the money that you need to purchase marketing materials, signage, business cards and inventory. Next you will find a checklist so that you can mark off every time you complete one of the steps from this chapter. Once your list is all checked off its official! You are a business owner!

Business Essentials Checklist

- o   Register Trade Name
- o   Get Tax ID number
- o   File Articles of Organization
- o   Establish Bank Account
- o   Create Email address

- o   Create Social Media sites
- o   Create logo
- o   Design Website

Chapter 6: How to Get More Money

Now that you have established your business it is time to find out how you can get some more money. In an ideal scenario your credit score is 800 and you are set. However, most likely you're like me and you have beat your credit to a bloody pulp. First you must start by finding out what your credit score is. There are free websites that will give you an estimate of what your credit score is across the 3 different credit reporting agencies. I personally use creditkarma.com. I have heard that credit Karma does not give an exact credit score however I believe it does get close to what your credit score is. When figuring out what type of funding you can get for your business you need to look at your credit score and determine what you would be eligible to receive as a startup. If you already know that you do not have good credit, once again do not worry, I will be covering multiple other ways that you can acquire the funding you need. They may require more work or time, but they will ultimately all get you to your goal of launching your business.

    Your first option is to get a business loan. If your credit is above a 620 then the chances are there is some type of loan or line of credit that you can receive. If you have set up your business bank account, you can try your bank first. Ask them about their line of credit or loan options. Banks have more stringent policies when it comes to giving out loans, so it may help if your score is higher than a 650. There are various other websites that will give out start up loans based on your credit score. You must be careful when it comes to getting a loan because there are a ton of fraudulent websites out there. I have filled out forms only to find out it was for a site that wanted to get my information, so they could call me 300 times a day about nonsense. Be careful and try to research the companies you put your information into.

Try to search on the SBA small business association website to find loans as well. You must also be smart when trying to get funding. If you do not need 20,000 do not try to get such a large amount. Most places will offer loan amounts up to $5000 with flexible payment options that allow you to pay your loan off over years. Make sure that you know exactly how much your monthly payment would be for your loan because you do not want to acquire a bill that you cannot pay. You also want to know how long it will take you to start making money once you launch your business because if you have a loan payment and your business isn't bringing in any money, you still will nee to make that payment.

One of my first business ideas was a cupcake food truck. I found a company that would pay for my build out costs if I put down 10% of the cost. The problem was that the truck could take up to 6 months to completely customize. I would have needed to make payments on my loan for at least 5 months before my truck would even be ready to get on the road and start making money. I had to reevaluate my entire business plan because I knew there would be no way I would be able to afford that extra bill. I also did not have the 10% to put down on the loan. Some places will require you to put down a percentage to obtain your funds.

If your credit score is not at a level that would allow you to get a loan, you have other options available to you. Evaluate your resources. Prepare a business pitch and see if anyone in your family would be able to give you a personal loan. Do you know anyone that may have the money that you need? Make sure you only ask for exactly what you need and be able to explain what the money will be used for in detail. If there is no one in your immediate circle that would be able to help you then crowdfunding may be a better fit for you. Before you move on to crowdfunding I want you to take a minute to remind yourself that it is OK if your loved ones can not help you. I remember being devastated when I could not turn to my family for help. I started being resentful when I saw family members going on vacations while simultaneously telling me they could not donate $1 towards my business. The thing that you must remember is that you can not demand help from anyone. While it may be discouraging to find out that you do not have the support that you were expecting, it will ultimately make you stronger and make you fight harder for your dream. Do not take the lack of support personally. Most entrepreneurs will tell you that they were surprised to learn that strangers will support you before your family or friends will.

Crowdfunding is another alternative to asking for help from the public to support you and your business. There are websites such as GoFundMe.com that allow users to create a campaign and raise funds to help them towards a cause. Make sure that you are aware of the terms and conditions associated with a service before starting your campaign. Some sites will require you to reach your overall goal before you will be allowed to cash out your funds. If you do not believe you will be able to raise $5000 it may be smarter to ask for a smaller amount like $1500 or an amount you feel will be easier to reach.

You should also lay out in your campaign exactly what you would like to do with the money you raise and do not be afraid to tell your personal story to get people interested in your success. There are other business crowdfunding sites that will allow you to offer people who donate an incentive. For example, you may be able to offer everyone who donates a coupon for your product when it launches. If you're like me this idea seems like something you would never do. I flat out refused to beg strangers for money in the beginning. My pride was in the way of me putting myself out there. I have to be honest with you guys crowdfunding was not successful for me. This method will always depend on who you reach with your campaign and who is willing to donate to your cause so this money is never guaranteed.

Finding a partner for your business may be something you would want to investigate when starting out, however this solution is by far the riskiest decision. If you know someone who has been looking to start a business as well or who you know you could join forces with and make your business a success, then go for it! The reason this solution is risky is because this person must be a good fit for you and your business. You MUST be able to trust this person with literally your life (or at very least your money). You must also be prepared to split profits with your partner which may be hard if there are no profits to split. Make sure your potential partner is willing to contribute equally what you have contributed. If your partner contributes less to the business make sure you have a contract in place that states that your partner will be getting a smaller percentage of profits for investing a smaller amount. There are legal documents such as partnership agreements online that can be downloaded and printed for you to sign with your partner. It may be beneficial to have a lawyer look over all contracts to ensure everyone is treated fairly. Going into a business partnership is like a marriage and that marriage can be very hard to get out of after you're already in. Do not attempt to find a partner if you do not want to compromise or listen to other ideas or be willing to change some of your policies to accommodate the ideas of your new partner. Finding a partner may be ideal for some however for me getting a partner almost ruined my business and my ability to trust anyone. I am sharing my story so that you are aware of what to look out for and how to protect yourself from potentially shady people.

When I first started looking for a retail store I contacted a real estate agent to view a storefront property. When I arrived at that property the agent had another woman come in to look at the property as well. I listened to this woman telling the agent she already had another location and was looking to open a second location. I left that property feeling very defeated because I assumed that the property would automatically go to her because she was more established. As I walked outside the woman approached me to ask what I do. I told her I made decorated cakes and she told me she had been looking for a partner because she baked but she did not decorate. After talking with her I followed her to her store so that we could talk further about how we could possibly benefit from each other. While at her store we both cried together, prayed together, and thought that God had sent us both the answer to our prayers. This woman had a commercial kitchen space as well as a store front location. She told me that because she was already established, she wanted me to buy into her company. The agreement was that I would pay her 10% or her overall profits for the previous year for me to become 50% owner of the business, and we would open a second location together. I thought that this was the best option for me because at the time I felt as if I needed this help. I was new to what I was doing and allowed her fast talking to cloud my judgement. I eventually gave this woman over $4000. I immediately quit my job and started working with her. After about a month of helping her make orders, decorating cakes for her, and working her store FOR FREE, I started wondering when we would be getting profits from the business.

I started seeing red flags, but I ignored them because we had built what I thought was a great working relationship. I started to notice that none of my ideas were taken seriously. When I wanted to try out a new cake she would brush me off. When I would ask for access to the finances she would give me the run around. She eventually gave me access to her PayPal account, but I still did not have full access to see what she was spending money on and why we were making money but not getting paid ourselves. When I did ask these questions, she became very defensive and confrontational. After feeling very uneasy I decided to dig deeper into the finances and found out that she had lied about the profits she had made for the previous year. In her PayPal account I saw that the overall sales she had for the year were very similar to the exact amount she told me was her profits. To make a long story short, she had me pay her for 10% of her SALES and not her profit. I still to this day have never seen an expense report to see where the money was going or if the business was even profitable.

The last straw for me was when we found our second location. We found out that the down payment for the location would be around $3500. To my knowledge I had just given this woman $4000 2 weeks prior, so I thought that we were still on the right track to opening another location. That same day she came to me to tell me we would need to do a bake sale and try to raise money for the deposit. This is when I had to lose it! How on earth is it possible that this woman had spent my $4000 in a matter of 2 weeks. She could not explain to me where my money had gone, where any of the money coming into the store had gone, or where any of the money for the cakes I decorated had disappeared to. That day we had a huge blow up and I packed up my belongings and took them back to my home. I felt completely betrayed and taken advantage of. This woman was not apologetic at all and in fact she tried to make it seem like I was being difficult for the questions I was asking. I had signed a contract for 50% ownership of her business and she never even disclosed her finances to me which was clearly laid out in the contract.

I asked her if she would return my money that I gave her, and I would dissolve the partnership and we could go our separate ways and she refused! I had no other choice but to take this woman to court to try to sue for my money back. In my lawsuit I clearly laid out which parts of the contract she had breached including lying about the amount for my buy in and not disclosing all business information to me. The contract stated that any amount over $500 being spent would need to be decided on between both partners and I had no idea where any of my money had gone. This woman obviously had plans of scamming me out of my money and hoped I would never catch on. The worst part about this entire ordeal was that I never got my money back. She filed for bankruptcy the day before we had to go to court and she listed me as one of her creditors. She had a lawyer send me a letter saying that if I came after her for any of my money she could turn around and sue ME. Not even a month later this woman was opening another store.

    I learned so much by going through that experience. I was completely discouraged that the progress I thought I had made was snatched away in an instant and I was back at square one. The reason that I feel I fell for such a scam was because I did not fully believe in myself or my gifts. When I think back on it I probably would have been just fine opening that original location by myself, but I thought I wasn't ready. By telling myself that I needed someone I allowed someone to grow their business with my hard-earned money. If there is one piece of advice I can give to you it is DO NOT allow someone to come into your business for their own personal benefit. Be cautious of everyone! This woman tricked me into thinking she was religious and even prayed and cried with me. Sometimes people are very good actors and when it comes to your business, you must make the right choices to avoid the situation I was in.

That year I had gotten the $4000 that I paid to my previous partner by filing my taxes and using my tax return. I knew that this was the only time throughout the year that I would have a large lump sum of money to invest into my business. I would eventually get another job and waited A WHOLE YEAR until the next tax time came around. Tax refunds are usually used for frivolous things like shopping, vacations or the things we normally cannot get throughout the year. Instead of using your tax return to buy furniture or new clothes why not use that money to invest in your business? The next year I got enough money back to be able to put a down payment on the store I currently have. During the year that I was working, I was still working my business as well. I drove for Lyft and uber, I delivered groceries through Instacart, I worked at a warehouse overnight, and I made my cakes. I did what I had to do to survive until I had enough money to make my business happen.

That leads me to the last alternative to getting your business started and that is to just start. Do you have enough money to make your first sale? Use the money from that first sale to make your next sale. Baking cakes at home I did not need any start up costs to make my first sale. I simply received money to make the customers cake and saved the remaining profit. When I noticed that I had a little money saving up I would invest that money into other things I needed such as cake pans, decorating tools and supplies. A cake might have required me to buy a certain size cake pan but I would make sure that I could get that new pan with the money the customer paid for their order. Depending on what your business is, it may be possible that the money you accept from customers will be enough to sell your product and receive some sort of profit. That profit should automatically be saved to go towards the business. This method will require you to work hard to grow your business form the ground up. Your profits should be added to the money you already have saved and go directly into your business bank account. It may take you a year or more to have enough money to make your next step for your business, but you will be in business!

Chapter 7: Launch!

Do you have what it takes to withstand the roller coaster ride you are about to get on? Starting a business is a huge risk. You may go through this entire book and start a business only for that business not to work out. You may have to make changes to your original plans as you learn more about what you've gotten into. Mentally you will constantly be tested, and you must have a strong sense of determination or you will crumble under the pressure. It is important to have the right mindset. You cannot be indecisive, you cannot wait around for the perfect time, you must LEAP!

Most entrepreneurs will tell you that your life will seem like its falling apart during this process. You may feel like you are under attack the moment you make your first step and that is normal. Everything that can go wrong WILL go wrong. The same day that I signed the lease for my new store my car got repossessed. A few weeks later my car was parked outside my store and was towed while I was inside working. I had to pay over $500 to get my car out of impound the day before my first store rent was due. I got into a car accident and injured my hip and had to go to physical therapy. All the equipment that came with my store started breaking and needed replaced one by one. It felt like there was one disaster after another falling into my lap. Had I not gone through everything that I had been through I most likely would have given up and went back to work. It is important for you to prepare yourself to be discouraged, disappointed, and defeated.

If you feel you have what it takes mentally physically and emotionally, then it is time for you to launch. This means that you are officially ready to start making your first sales. Start posting on your social media pages and start advertising. Facebook and Instagram both have options for you to pay money to boost your posts. It could cost you as little as $5 to get your posts seen by thousands of people. Utilize these marketing strategies to get your business out there. Boosting your post allows you to pick a demographic that you want to target and get your posts to. You can pick a certain distance a certain age group and even males or females specifically. Facebook also has a marketplace that allows people to post what they have for sale. Do not be afraid to post constantly. The only way that you will get the publics attention is to reach them. We all know those sites that we want to unfollow because they are the only posts on our timeline, be like them!

When you make your first sale try to take a picture. People like to see that other people are shopping with you. Take a picture of someone holding your bag or wearing your products. Have other people that you know repost things for you to reach their friend list as well. This is not the time to be lazy and think that customers will fall into your lap you have to bring the customers in. If you have ordered business cards you should always keep them with you. Give your card to everyone and do not be afraid to speak to strangers. Not everyone will be interested in what you have to offer but it cannot hurt to stop people on the street, introduce yourself and give them your card. That person may not need your services, but they know someone who does.

Now that you have prepared yourself and gone through all the steps necessary, you should be ready to run a successful business. Remember the skills you have learned throughout this book because you will need all of them as you walk on this journey. Your budgeting and time management skills will be essential to making your business profitable. The same budgeting that you did while saving for your business you should do with your actual business income. Do not be frivolous with money, only purchase what you need and let your money grow before making large purchases. Be mindful of your time and be careful of overworking yourself. Know the signs of you becoming burned out and try to avoid becoming exhausted.

Broke Girl Tip: The last tip that I have for you may be the most important one and that is: DO NOT QUIT YOUR DAY JOB! It is better to have the added income than it would be for you to struggle to pay your household bills as well as your business bills. Until your business is bringing in enough profit to sustain your household expenses you should remain working your full-time job. I personally jumped out there and quit my job WAY too soon.   Had I remained at my fulltime job I would not have needed to take business money and put it directly into my household without being able to invest it back into my business. The added struggle may cause you to want to give up sooner than you would have had you had another income to fall back on.

Always remember that this is only the beginning for you. This business could lead you to expanding and growing your business into a huge empire! You may also realize you want to try your hand at multiple businesses and open as many as you can handle. The choice is yours! It is possible to end the cycle of poverty and change your circumstances and I hope that this book has helped you to

realize that your possibilities and potential are ENDLESS!
Thank you for reading and GOOD LUCK!!